C000244553

Extinction
Rebellion

A Tribute

Mike Johnson

Extinction Rebellion

A Tribute

Press

99% Press,
an imprint of Lasavia Publishing Ltd.
Auckland, New Zealand

www.lasaviapublishing.com

Copyright © Mike Johnson, 2020

Cover design by Jennifer Rackham, 2020

This book is copyright. Apart from any fair dealing
for the purpose of private study, research, criticism
or reviews, as permitted under the Copyright Act, no
part may be reproduced by any process without the
permission of the publishers.

ISBN: 978-0-9951282-2-4

We have just 12 years to make massive and unprecedented changes to global energy infrastructure to limit global warming to moderate levels, the United Nation's climate science body said in a monumental new report released Sunday.

"There is no documented historic precedent" for the action needed at this moment, the Intergovernmental Panel on Climate Change (IPCC) wrote in its 700-page report on the impacts of global warming of 2.7 degrees Fahrenheit, or 1.5 degrees Celsius.

From rising sea levels to more devastating droughts to more damaging storms, the report makes brutally clear that warming will make the world worse for us in the forms of famine, disease, economic tolls, and refugee crises.

vox.com

You must abandon poetry before it abandons you

Bill Manhire

Livesong

ant and eggshell

the surface I walk upon
is a very pale blue
with tiny specks
where stars died

and it's curved too
rather beautifully

it's a structural miracle
the magic ovoid
in which movement quickens

everywhere I walk
is an unfolding horizon
always new

when I pause
it's to get my bearings
and when I turn my head to one side
it's to get a feel for the other
and the distant heartbeat of something
I can't even conceive

livesong

it comes with certain mornings
before memory
in what the children call
the early world
when the light is diffused
in such a way
as to be
more fluid than shade

airy as a lover's touch
grazing the underside of a leaf
with pastels
slipping sideways
whispering through caverns of shadow
before birth, before time ticked
and the livesong was
everything that was
or needed to be
whilst the morning stands eternal
against light's passing

and the livesong lives on
wound through
the twilight of the living
and the dead

they

from here and there
and all over
everywhere
out of the woodwork
out of the shadows
out of the past
out of memory and desire
love and joy
delight and torment
and the mortality of angels

they creep forth
to gather
bearing a hard truth
still looking
for a home in the world

liar liar

liar, liar
pants on fire
nose as long as a
telephone wire

your brains aren't worth
a worn out tire

confess! confess!
to the great unholy mess

it's pretty dry now
and will soon be gettin' drier

to a friend in Beijing

living in a shroud
of soot
and filthy smudge
and desperate mirages

how can I write you
any kind of melody
as you can go for months
and never see a star
nor even a trace of the moon
but for a dull glow
overridden by neon and halogen
and rapid talk

there is so much noise
you are cut off from
the music of the spheres
those grand themes we find
in a whispering forest
or on the edge of a clean tide
or deep in the harmonies of ice

you must witness young children
coughing up their lungs
in sad hospitals
with sad windows
while the weather gets hotter
and the air begins to burn
with a chemical smell
and life becomes more and more
unlikely, impossible
conjectural
with everybody living for some
imagined future
or in some imagined past

it's a far cry, is it not, from how
we used to be, back in the day
when the sky ran open
and we did too
up the back roads and
along the river beds
you must remember
you have to remember

in the end
it comes down to language
the language of melody

the time signatures of forests and streams
children laughing in effervescent waters
the beat and metre of unfettered skies
cool air in the lungs
the contralto flash of a blackbird or a thrush
across an open window
the back beat
of trees green and dolphins blue
the clippings from bird song at dawn
or the sudden silence, the pause,
of a moment that becomes itself
and nothing more

if I were to write such a song
I might as well be writing of centaurs
and cyclopes, fauns and dryads
and three-headed dogs
and gypsy flowers
and fairy dust
for all its meaning to you
and what you see from your window

I might as well go hug a tree
and forget about all the rest

I can barely conceive what song must be like

for you, when all common referents

even the skies above and earth below

have been obliterated

and there are no spirits around

to make merry of the dawn

or streak your windows with sly colours

or a wind to touch your face with silk

how could I sing into your heart

or stir your spirit for the dance

let alone make you laugh

or cry

the pathos of poetry

just in from India
a record breaking hurricane
a million people displaced

a struggle to put back a life
that will never be replaced

all over the globe, the same story

the dry gets drier, the wet wetter
oceans rip into coastlines
heat surges rip open oceans

I doubt these people
have much time for fancy lines

poetry can never become
the privilege of the protected
and the powerful
for it is always there, present
in the voiced grief and bitter hopes
of the survivors

grieve while you can for the old magic

grieve
for the mountains
and the sky
and the ocean
and all that is lost
and being lost
to us
as the old magic
drains from the land

turn wheel turn
how the fires burn

grieve
for all that lives and moves
and asks only to live
and move
with the larger movement
of the living and the breathing
as the old magic
fades
and death starts to stink

to high heaven

turn wheel turn
how the fires burn

grieve for paradise lost
even as your tears
dry up
and your cheeks crack open
and there's nothing left to drink
that doesn't stick in your craw

grieve for grief itself
as sorrow truly tragic
belongs to the old magic
to the catharsis of joy
but grief and its attendants
have fled
or been put behind bars
or sent to war

soon
there will be merely a hollow place
where grief once ruled
in all its trappings

and nobody will remember
what tears are for

lost world

trees that stood straight and tall
made a bid for the sky
and filled the air with scent
now lean drunkenly
or turn into ghosts that have
forgotten everything
except their mineral bones
and the stories their leaves once told
to the wind

bread that once nourished the blood
and gladdened the heart
now barely feeds the flesh
a promise hollow and empty

wine that warmed the belly
and staggered the mind
now smells of smoke
and tastes like an overripe sun
or vinegar tears

earth, that once basked
in its cool places

refreshing frosts
and shadowy dreams
now bakes or turns to slush

words, that once came crisp
and clean off the page
or from the hollow caverns
of the body
fade in the mouth, and choke
for want of space
to breathe

and for music we cannot say
for we have cast away
the original sound
from which all other sounds play
that note of grace

forfeited, and now hidden
the world we have lost

ten years

ten years to go
money to blow
nothing to show

ten short years long
we're all gone

pack the bong

they first to die

nobody gets it all
unless it's all there
to get

hard to put a planet
in your pocket
along with everything else

all that pride
takes up a lot of space

when it's all or nothing
the nothing is all
you end up
with empty pockets

and a planet that's not much use
to anybody
anymore

nobody gets it all
and some don't get any of it
they die first

autumn

it's not yet as hot
as it could be
as it will be
as it has to be

we pop on our coats
we rub our hands
wipe some condensation
off the glass

the sun gets in a brief look
between showers

grateful we are
for that cool southerly wind

blowing off the ice

the intention

I'm in alpine territory
above the tree line
the last clump of birch

I can follow the intention
of the hills, all the way down
to distant green
or back up towards
the promise of snow

moss and rock cling
gravity glides
wind scars the slopes
the sky turns dark honey

there is no horizon
earth and sky just overlap
lips joined in open secrecy

I can lie down here, go soft
on the hard rock
and let the mountain do the dreaming

geologic moment: Tongariro

the lava flow broke off here
you can see
where the hillside
drops off sheer
to the folds of the valleys

you can stand at the very spot
where the blood tide of molten rock
oozed to a stop

we're in the land of mosses
lichens and liverworts

trees are a distant thought
and life is just something
that gets in under the fingernails

as we lived

our history will be written in rock
in the fossil records
in broken landscapes
and plastic filled oceans

the planet itself
will be our memorial
and our obituaries will be carved
from violent skies
and a shimmering heat haze

a short-lived species, as species go
for as we lived, we died

the sentry

I've been standing watch
since the day it was announced
that our world was going to die
if we didn't stop
blowing each other up
mowing each other down
and heating up the air

there's no future in it
for the living or the dead

already my feet are strangers
to my mind
and I hardly know
who it is I'm watching out for
or why

everybody seems so normal

nobody looks like a criminal
or a mass murderer
and the barbarians all have suits
and revolving doors

my eyes grow opaque
and the dark is coming down
but there's no relief in sight
no echo of any footfall

no one else to keep watch
through the night

and no one to declare
a universal armistice

Anzac Day 2019

those guns have fallen silent
or at least fooled us into thinking so

the dead have stayed dead
or been very quiet about it

the land has repaired itself with flowers
or failed to do so

the mourners have gone back to their lives
or think they have

but, quite close by it seems
the war rumbles on regardless

mimic

we have it all wrong

it boasts a human body
feeds a beating heart
wears a human face

uses words that sound
just like ours

we mistake it for one of us
its camouflage is so perfect
nobody notices a thing

everybody wants in on the action
when there is a killing to be made
nobody hears the worm turn

when it takes off its face
we know it for what it is

we don't have to look twice

how worser

how bad does it have to get
we ask

from bad to badder
and worse than we ever imagined

the big heat and the big die off
the big hatred and the big pretend
isn't that bad enough

everyday we hide our faces
from each other
as it goes from bad to worse
and from worse to worser

still we ask
in as many voices as we can muster
how bad does it have to get?

it doesn't balance

the idea that everything balances out
in the end
doesn't balance out

supersymmetry is not so super

in fact, I'd say
things go out of whack
pretty damn quick

I'd like to think that these words
balance out the wordless

that there is a duet of night and day
a counterpoint of lines and spaces

that when someone is crying
someone else is laughing
but really, this is no laughing matter
and those carrying the burden
are running out of tears

I'd like to think
there is an even handedness
in the fall of a leaf
but the leaf just falls
and when the forest falls
the leaves all fall at the same time
revealing an empty sky

I'd like to join those who believe
that a great judgment will come down
upon the heads of the guilty
but it's just wishful thinking

I'd like to think of these things
as weighed on the scales
of some cosmic equity
but it really just doesn't balance out

and I'm feeling, way, way
way off center

baby boomer speaks

we are the ones who saw
our hopes for a better world
eaten away
to nothing
in the name of progress

not a better world
but a worse one
a worse one by far
beyond our dystopian imaginings

sister! how come we're all riding
the algorithms of doom?

brother, where have all
the pastures of plenty gone?

Oh mother
will ours be
The first of the last generations?

still waiting

I've been waiting here
an eternity
for something to show

but that's about it
decency turns the other way

and by the time something shows
the show's over

the cosmos has turned
back into an egg
scrolls have rolled up the stars
rocks have surrendered their fire
and even late night footsteps
have turned for home

it doesn't pay to wait, pumpkin
it takes too damn long

soft bandage

when a little gentle rain falls
we make amends

the first shall be last and the last
shall be first
we tell each other

it sounds good that way
a little green springs up
in our mind's eye
a little opening in the heart
to let the truth in
a soft bandage to the wound

we may not have the morrow
but we have the day
we tell ourselves

and the day has just begun

a new syndrome

I think I've got
hyper-stimulation-future-shock fatigue
it's a new syndrome
I just invented it
to explain how I'm feeling
and why my body is screwing up

I want to put my anchor down
in the real world
but I can't find it – the world I mean

the world that hides behind
all that jitteriness
and barely swallowed fear

I think the real world
is another false news story
but that just goes to show
so help me
what a grip this syndrome has
how deadly it can be
if not properly contained

and it's not getting any easier
to concentrate
with a mind that
slides off in all
directions
following will-o-wisps
into the galaxies of nowhere

there's no cure for
hyper-stimulation-future-shock fatigue
but it can be managed with the correct doses
of anti-inflammatory language
and love-peace-and-sisterhood

I don't know why it is that my pots and pans
turn into plots and plans
or why I get muddled with the sounds between
and find it hard to talk in the syntax
of common sense

things will only get more skittish and edgy
which is about the only thing
I can anticipate with any confidence

lines running backwards

nothing
will come to

and all your projects, plans and policies
a world of vanishing futures
at least in this world
problem is, there may be no future
it all looks pretty good on paper
at least for you
when everything comes right
as we will be
it's all very well to imagine ourselves
if possible
for your children
and accumulating a little something
avoiding taxes
plotting and hatching schemes
to spend many hours
it's all very normal
everybody does
to make plans for the future
it's all very well

the same world

after the floods, everything grew
fast and rank

then

dried back, died back
and turned to tinder

each morning, we sniff the air
just to make sure
we're in the same world

overheard at Mt Eden bus stop

too much of a good thing
is a bad thing
apparently

never thought I'd hear
anybody complain
about how nice the weather is
even this far into autumn

but there you go
no satisfying some people

hell, if it gets too hot
open a window

let's not panic

the climate's not changing
it's just the weather

sea levels are not rising
it's just erosion

the land is not drying out
it's just seasonal variation

a year's rain in one day
is a one in a hundred year event

and if I seem to be wrong
it's just because

everyone else is lying

cartoon

the fat cat sits in the back
of his limo
and rolls up all his darkened windows

but he knows, he's seen the data
he's grasped the trend-lines
he's gone knuckle to knuckle with bar-graphs

he's faced what there is to face
he comprehends the nature of his ruin
as he has never comprehended anything
in his whole life

now he sees with uncluttered vision

with all the courage he can muster
he taps his driver on the shoulder
'drive over the cliff, James,' he says
 'I'm committing suicide'

extinction rebellion

her name is Blythe Pepino
she is a real person
a flesh and blood person
with flesh and blood hopes and dreams
who, against her deepest wishes
has decided not to have any children
because of "climate breakdown
and civilisation collapse"

my heart goes out to Blythe Pepino
and her partner
and their unborn children
whose lives are forfeit
before they are even conceived
to those who have too much
already

and if Blythe Pepino should wake one night
to the sound of a child crying for comfort
she should allow herself to grieve
and grieve wholly
for the generations of suffering
are coming to an end

Greta Thunberg

the child who cried wolf
got into a lot of trouble
when there was no wolf

the whole village got stirred up
all for nothing

the child is still in trouble
because the village is now crying 'no wolf'
when the wolf is obviously
at the gate

and only the child can see it

profit and loss

disaster capitalism will lead
to one final disaster
one ultimate market cataclysm

potential profits are staggering
but can never be realized

there's no future
to stack the futures up against

everybody else will go broke
and scratch in the ground
to grow potatoes
with one fearful eye
on the weather

brain damage

some black snake has taken a bite
out of the moon

some maggoty hand
has taken hold of the earth

some bitter song
has crept into our throats

a dead humming noise
has taken over the night

a nameless stench
saturates the wind

twisted words
writhe on our screens

and we can't think straight
any
more

neonicotinoids

when bees die people die
it's not that hard to work out
Einstein had it figured

a combination of global heating
and neonicotinoids
with names like acetamiprid, clothianidin,
imidacloprid, nitenpyram, nithiazine,
thiacloprid and thiamethoxam
does the trick

marinate the environment in nicotine
then apply heat, wet or dry

the humble bees don't stand a chance
nor does much else

I'm with Extinction Rebellion

why join the queues shuffling their way
to a passive death
like holocaust victims to the gas chambers

why watch the world die
for the privilege of the few
who know no shame
deny, defer, and denigrate
and then apportion blame

get a grip on yourself
join the young who refuse to die
quietly

sit down
sit down in front of the machine
stop the machine

let's bring everything to a great
grinding halt

let the traffic snarl
let the cops cop

let the judges judge
let the fools fool

let everything out
in one big shout

backdrop

the climate crisis
has now become the backdrop
to everything

all our dramas
all our personal stuff
all our precious
subjectivity

all our most wonderful
theories of everything
and intimate sense
of everything else

is going up in flames
or down in the flood

so why bother, you ask
why bother the already bothered

because that's what we do

when stuck on the end of a pin
we wriggle

the terraformers

they talk about going to Mars
Mars is the place to be
they don't have to

they are busy right now
turning Earth into Mars

response team

they were there
lines and lines of them
stretching into the distance

they came with their hands out
they came with their hearts sore
they came with their bodies broken

so we cut off their hands
ate their hearts
and buried their bodies
before they were properly dead

because we told ourselves
over and over
that we didn't care

at your door

we are the lost ones
the missed ones
the disappeared
displaced

the harder you look
the less visible we are

the less visible we are
the more our presence is felt

the more our presence is felt
the more we are pushed
to one side

the more we are pushed
the closer we crowd

madness lies
just around the corner
where you will find us

staring right back at you

it's official

no, earth won't wink out of sight
caught in a wrinkle in time-space

it won't go up in a ball of flame
like a rag soused in oil

it won't go down to the roar
of the very last wave

people won't fall over dead
in the middle of the street

no god will appear
waving a big stick

in fact, we'll hardly notice a thing

and yet
we will have passed
that invisible mark in time
that final tipping point
the point of no return
beyond which

civilization becomes impossible
and humans will go down dying

looks so bald, just written down like that
with no frills, no supporting imagery
to comfort the mind
no turn into a supporting phrase
but we shouldn't be surprised
nearly every species that has ever existed
has become extinct
it's in the record
those crocodiles and cockroaches
are the exception that proves the rule

so by 2030
our doom will have become
inescapable
because we failed to act

but not much else will change
I expect
we'll have got used to the idea by then

massive heist

it is the most massive heist
the world has ever seen

a job of breathtaking scope
and daring

they stole the whole fucking planet

much rather

I'd much rather do something else
like eat a strawberry

I'd much rather think about something else
like the girl next door

I'd much rather set my sights
on something nice
like a cool summer cruise to the Antarctic

I'd much rather love the love I love
than look around for another planet

I'd much rather have the time
to take the time, thank you
than be rushed off my feet
going nowhere fast

I'd much rather be
the idiot I am, than have to be wise
and see what I'd rather not see

I'd much rather sleep than have to wake
to another day in the slow death of life

I'd much rather write for the glory of god
than pen weather reports
for those who don't read them

I'd much rather join the saints
than be a sock puppet covered in blood

I'd much rather celebrate
than have to bury the baby
in a cracked garden

I'd much rather be happy
than pack a sad

but here we are, where we are
and what we'd rather like

pretty much counts for jack shit

less said

the less said
the soonest mended?
I don't think so

take another look

who I am

I'm pretty much stuck
with who I am and
where I am

and what I can divine

never thought it would go down this fast
or this hard

see you soon sucker

I asked them to come around
to talk to me, comfort me
tell me this has all happened before
and every generation
becomes its own apocalypse

life goes on, the world keeps turning
no matter which way you look
and the poor will always be with you
the book says, which means
the empire will always be with us
and soldiers will never be far from the streets

but my ancestors have gone on holiday
maybe it got too hot for them, or they finally
got sick of the world
and my so-called spirit guides
are not much better, having, it seems
abdicated the field for fresher climes
and left me with a note that says
cultivate the self
or maybe it says, see you soon sucker

I don't blame them for getting out in time
out of line, for their sorrow
for their pleading, for their profound
absence

because the dead need a living world
as much as we do

no longer the sun

no longer those majestic
shafts of light you'll find
in the arched spaces of cathedrals
falling like a blessing
on the land and the people

no longer that zen glimpse
of a hidden garden
suffused with a soft glow
and damp vines of green
and sugary fruit

but rather
a terrible eye that never shuts
that levers open skies
where the light is always hard
and soft things wither away
and stones crack open
in dried river beds

a new sun has been born
pitiless, ferocious
the new god of refugees

deus-ex-machina

once we could say, as a comforting truth
that while we lived and fought and died
and visited good and evil upon each other
all the rest would stand
                    that the sky
the ocean and the land
and all that may be evoked with our sacred breath
would be eternal
above and beyond our petty, murderous selves
always there to bring lilacs
to a broken land

that spring would come and creep through
the barbed wire, and autumn turn
deciduous forests into one swathe of
yellow and orange
and that winter fires light the heart

these comforts have gone

spring comes too early, too late
or not at all, summer turns autumn
into summer, forests turn into a swathe

of flame

while nothing is the same, sky

earth and sea

have joined the drama, not as backdrop

or as a Greek chorus

or even a character in a mask

but as *deus-ex-machina*

sweeping the action aside

in one great gesture

a solution to an intractable plot

consequences

we have played the game of consequences
and lost

we thought it didn't matter
we thought that there was more
where that come from
lots more

we didn't connect the dots
no matter how many
piled up

by that time we didn't give a rat's arse
about what lived and what died
as long as we hogged as much of it
as we could
before it was all gone

we turned our hearts to stone
and our souls to little wind up toys
that needed rewinding all the time
though propaganda and tricks
of the mind

we became incapable of perceiving
consequences and so
incapable of dealing with them

it's very simple really
after a time, we just ran out of time
and the consequences
came rolling in

hung out to dry

as we neared the top of the hill
the sky regained its force
the earth embraced its own
delicious curve
and stars proclaimed their clarity

the world of us and them
and everyone else
fell away
just for a moment

you know
the way these things go

it all seemed
as if it were meant to be

when we got the top
it was all there
receding into thought and distance
landscape and memory

we went into a bit of a trance
we didn't say it, but it was
in front of us

a world hung out to dry

# of pens and swords

in this situation, the pen
is hardly mightier than the sword
although it tries to be

we understand that all wars
are wars of the mind
sword or pen

the pen is double-edged
while the sword cannot cut the word
only air and flesh

and prayers may be heard
by the wrong gods

even if they are not spoken

something else

you can't stop progress
they said

and that sounded right
even though it was wrong

and even when it turned out
to be something else
we still didn't stop it

and kept calling it progress

the sedulous ape

like any kind of thought
it reaches saturation point

there's only so much
the monkey brain can take

confused by the consequences
forgetting the sequences
confusing the frequencies

we keep hitting ourselves
with the same rock, wondering
what's causing the pain
blaming god, or better still
the other guy

hell, we won't get far that way

better to empty the bucket
on the fire
than step in it

forget the rest

from here on
it's nature that's calling the shots
not us, not our bots
we've shot our shots
we've shot the lot

no use pretending that geo-politics
lies at the heart of things
that's last century's game

the chessboard world
the rise and fall of politicians
the clash of ideologies
nationalist passions
and neo-con scams

now war and civil war are driven
by hot winds, dying lands
plague dreams
and the sudden floods that turn
into people

as crops fail

the water holes dry up
and babies wail

as the skies turn to glass
as the hurricanes make their landing

and cars bump and grind
down rivers of mud

it's pretty clear who is
and who isn't
in charge

providence

I don't see much providence
In the fall of a sparrow
or any other bird

I'm trying to take the larger view
that maybe when one garden withers
another flourishes
in an alternate time or space

I want to pretend
that there is some kind of even-handedness
in things
super-symmetry or whatever

humans may end their tenure
but earth must abide

except if it doesn't

there are dead and empty planets
aplenty
from gas giants to ice pebbles
to airless rocks

it wouldn't take much for earth
to join them
just a little push

a zombie planet, slipping through
the spacetime fabric
devoid of all but the memory
of something that stirred
in fresh winds

that there will be life beyond
the horizon of our instruments
as a matter of logic
is of little comfort

it's just buried somewhere in the mathematics
of enormous distances and
plunging time

I don't see much providence
In the fall of a planet

and a chance born out of miraculous odds
going nowhere

stealing flowers

whoever who stole flowers
out of time's garden
probably didn't know what they were doing
and ended up with wrinkled hands
failing eyes
and withered blooms

they just saw something bright
and beautiful
and reached out to touch
take
and break

one moment you're wandering along
with barely a care in the world
and a whistle in the air
next thing
you're carrying a bouquet of hours
still fresh
through the market place
where everything's for sale except a carefree
moment
and melodies are quickly forgotten

all those coveted flowers

will fade into the ancient faces of children

and miss their mark

hurtsville

I've got a headache from all this
the heat, the mess
the betrayal, the kiss
the whole sick crew
the chemical stew

all this running back and forward
to the piss pot
all this over the top, take a shot
have a screw

the malevolence that chases clouds away
and fills the streams with didymo
to block them up and choke the flow

all this plays crazy with my mind
circles me, squares me, jokers me
drops me into evil dreams

this headache bores a hole
in my head, and everything else
get left unsaid

the smart money's on trees

plant as many trees as you
can lay your hands on, buddy

good hardy ones with a strong faith
a deep root system
and nice fat leaves

it's a good one to one-and-half degrees
cooler
in the shade
under the canopy
and it won't be long
before this kind of cover
is worth its weight

in gold

heat spots

have you heard
there are heat waves
in the ocean

tsunamis of heat
turning the ocean
into a killing floor

you don't find
this kind of news
so easily
now the truth is out

it's too factual
it's too hard to spin
and can't be blamed
on Moslim terrorists
or eco-activists
or abortionists
or the Pope

have you heard?
have you heard?

spread the word

there are hot spots in the ocean
now
in which everything
dies

period

press the panic button

set the alarm
put a time limit on it

sleep is all very well, but
you can have too much of it

grief is all very well
but we have a surfeit of tears

anger is all very well
but there's been enough killing

set the alarm, and
sound the alarm

get yourself out of bed
take some deep breaths

let's do
what has to be done
quickly

evolution

if sharp claws survive
be a sharp claw

if it takes a mountain
to stay upright
be a mountain

show me the bird
that can build its nest in the air

show me the one that is
at one with the one
and I'll show you a world restored

if sharp claws don't do the trick
let them wither away

if the mountain can't take it
move the mountain

if it takes impossible love
then be impossible
and let's survive that way

at long last

there comes a point
right now, in fact
when words leave off
and action begins

we've had enough words
already
fools talking backwards

if words don't lead to actions
they fester
ask any lover

when words fail us
we fail ourselves

all those grand plans
are little better than a scam

so tomorrow we hit the streets
not to march
but shut down the beast

extinction rebellion is on the move

pass the word

Deadsong

what the dead dream

the dead dream of forests
rushing silences
and cavernous streams

the living dream of red meat
warm sex
and money in the bank

those in-between haven't learned
to dream yet

they know only the haphazard winds
the slipshod stars
the hasty cosmos

and the echo of make believe

you and I

you and I
we've seen our share of dawns
slipping between
the here and the there
the now and the then

you and I have had a fair go
you might say
done the rounds
shaken the sugar tree
stayed one step ahead of the sun

funny how slow
it's coming on this morning
bit by bit

I took a look outside myself
and hardly saw a glimmer
nothing that would lift the lid
on itself
and set itself free

it's not that we're waiting for anything
is it?

I've never seen a dawn yet
that held back
that could hold back
breaking day

you and I have to wonder, now
what happens next

the kingdom of deceit

we went over to the dark side
because the light got in the way

we hid our faces
when footsteps approached
we put our hands in our ears
when thunder clapped

some plausible, well-dressed people
told us we didn't have to think
for ourselves
or start connecting the dots
so we didn't
it was much easier that way
for a while

such a relief
to let other people
do all the thinking
for a while

if we covered out eyes
no one would see us
we thought

so we covered them
and the dark behind our eyes
was complete

if we cauterized our hearts
no one would hear them beating
we fervently believed

so we cauterized them
and the consolation was immediate

if we died quietly
we would enjoy a happy afterlife
we were assured

so we died quietly and here we are
with our apartment in the city of death

there was an answer to everything
and an answer to nothing
but we were too lazy to figure that one out
and besides
the drugs were really nice
and worked a wonder

so they stole our hands

our arms

our feet and our legs

our genitals

and our tongues

until there was nothing left of us

but chopped dreams

mass graveyards

and false memories

because that's what happens

on the dark side, in the land of slavery

in the kingdom of deceit

everything is offered

and everything is taken away

in the same moment

and freedom seems very far off

heat kills

the heat kills off the very young
and the very old first, they say

so being just born, I'm right
in the firing line
and being just dead, I remember it all
as it happened

in Aussie,
we have fruit cooking on the branch
from the inside out
neatly microwaved and ready to eat

bears falling out of trees
with bleeding eyes
birds falling out of the air
wings on fire
roads that twist 'n warp
fresh from a Salvador Dali painting

reservois that turn into cracked mud
dead animals that fall over
on their way to water

or lie clustered around a dry oasis
like a star made of bones

everywhere we look we see ourselves

really, I don't think I can make art
with these kinds of materials

I don't know why I'd want to
go there
but there you go

you work with what you've got
try to hold a mirror up to things
and then you find
that things are holding a mirror
up to a mirror

it's a hot day and promises to be
a hot night, restless and clammy

the heat, they say, kills off the young
and the old first, because their
inner thermostats don't work so good
and they can't regulate the blood
temperature

being one of the newly dead
it shouldn't affect me
however
this mind doesn't work
so good any more
and I can't be sure
if beauty is really truth
because the truth is no longer young

I keep up the good work anyway
as it's nice
to have something to do

in the fast lane

I had to go deep in
to where matter didn't matter
and was never matter anyway
so what the hell?

I had to go in
faster than the speed of light
faster than the speed of thought
past hologram projections
of multiple worlds
where people lived, unknowing
uncaring
past the two-faced judges
and half-faced gamblers
through all those mechanical dreams
and pokie machines
up and under
the other who was gunning for me
and down the other side
it was a helluva ride

until it all stopped one day
and I up and died

Deadsong

it's no great shakes being dead
while walking among the living

the living have a living to make
the dead have a past to shake

nobody's got one up
on anybody else
except in their head

I'm sorry if you can hear me at night
pacing about
in solemn footfall, the heavy tread
it's just that I have fears to counter
and while it seems like
my death is a fake
I can hardly face the daily dread

It's all mixed up now
nobody came first or second
nobody won and everybody lost
and nobody knows how

children got old before they lived
the old stayed old too long
and there was never enough blood
to go around

it's no great shakes being dead
while walking among the living

I can only see myself
In the passing glass of shop windows
and can only see the world
in the frightened eyes of the living

these few gestures will have to pass
for motion and meaning
a feel for the whole and the part

for a stake in the world
that doesn't go through the heart

the devil's walking parody

here in the afterworld,
I can wander with the dinosaur
the dodo and the mud-dragon
having lost it all
just like them

I reckon I've lost
what I never had
which is a funny feeling
like an extra limb that never was
or an eye that never learned
how to grow
or a wing that never knew
the art of feathers

fame and fortune pass by
from time to time
and all I do is tip my hat
to Wednesday
and carry on

they are always so busy
those twin sisters

with superior and important people
who seem, in hindsight
quite innocent of the nature of the world
how it comes and goes
tops and bottoms
and who gets shafted
in the end

love and affection come to visit
but I am never quite sure
when they will up and leave
with no goodbye
to look for another cave
in the mountains

I think I lost all the plots
except this one
(a mystery story, after all)
but I'm in good company
with all kinds of fantastic creatures
a bestiary of the outlandish
nature's genetic flings into the improbable
like wings too heavy to fly
or a carcass too big to feed
or a mind that lost control of greed

far too smart, but in the end
not smart enough

I feel quite at home
with nature's parodies
and I have no problem
when a bunch of dead
and ill-fitted birds
gather around to laugh at me

it's not worth doing something

dead men tell no tales
or so they say
but I wouldn't be too sure of that
I've heard a tale or two
from bare bones
and clacking teeth

mostly of daring
in the face of overwhelming odds

the stories the dead tell
are all cautionary by nature
none of them have the courage left
to propagate any lies
or bury the truth along with their bones

so
put your ear to the ground
and there's no telling what
you might hear
or read between the lines

they particularly want you
not to do what they did
the nature of which you may taste
in the particles of carrion
emerging from their mental cavities
like a host of ghost plagues
a visitation of funerals

but the dead tell tales all right
they'll speak out of turn
at every turn
steal the words right out of your mouth

they are total converts
to show don't tell
although a little show and tell
works just as well

stories arrive
from the deadlands beyond
the lowdown on the lowdown
the inside dope
what the dead say
when there's no one alive to hear

come! see the world
through our eyes for a while
go the extra mile
learn to smile
it's no good doing something

if it's not worthwhile

the book

the pages of the text
have blown away
or been stuck in the neck
of Molotov cocktails
soaked in accelerant

the paper was too thin
or
the words too frail
or
the glue came unstuck
or
everything just turned yellow
or
someone got the wrong
end of the stick

the binding was never designed
for the punishment
it is now taking

its pretentions look quite forlorn

and besides, the dead
don't read too good

hanged man and the tree of life

I saw the nine worlds
devoured by flame
and dark

for nine days I hung
upside down
and watched the carnage
through alien eyes

the worlds cooked like fruit on a branch
the constellations began to glow
and then the great tree itself
even the tree from which I dangled
began to crack and lean
and deep in the rock its roots
began to quiver

in nine days everything which
had been made

was unmade

the granite beast

when I unwake
clouds are piled on my eyelids
pillars of fire address my wounds
and history is buried
in some far away music
beyond the horizon

my blood has turned to surging algorithms
my hands are fractal images
of each other
my arms bend like a stick refracted in water
my legs seek their own direction
in a river of stones

a neutron star pulses
in each eye socket
and I exhale through a straw
into the void
and from the void
back into the body of me
or me as body
so the rivers might flow
and the forests grow

slime-mould appears
from my spinal cord
and the air is filled with luminous
jellyfish, undulating
like fashion models on a submarine
catwalk

when I look around
people come up to me out of their lives
and want to know
what the hell is going on
who came first
and who hasn't been paid

I think I know but say nothing
in case I say what I don't mean
or mean what I can't say
and end up in a tango

some things are better left unsaid
especially
when talking to the dead

when I stand up, the world apes me
everything acts like
a mirror to everything else

so nothing shows
but the reflections
and the glimmer of a hidden
light source

words are backing up
nobody wants to go that far
beyond belief
beyond the pale

when I walk, nothing moves
in relation to me
as you might expect
my feet are giddy with stars
my knees go clink-clank
the machinery of my soul
will dip and glide

and when I speak, my voice
goes off like depth charges placed
many miles deep
where the ocean is most dense
and dreams are infinite

in the whispering whirlwinds
below the theatre of sound

words are forming and unforming
being and nothingness

when I unwake
the destroyer of forms
unwakes with me
and all hell breaks loose

ghost story

as my foot hits the road
I can hear footfalls
echoing behind me

but I'm too scared
to turn around

especially as
those footfalls sound
just like mine

and there are enough of me here
already

I have to ask them to keep
to their own space and time
to keep their distance
and leave me alone in mine
but there's sweet chance of that
as with every step
those other steps
draw closer

not as dead

you're never quite as dead
as you think you are

you cut into your flesh
with a razor blade

the relief is instant
you bleed

but the songs of the dead return
with bleak insistence
and there is nothing you can do
nowhere you can go
to make anything feel any better

as long as I draw breath
you say
as you draw another
and another

among the living

at first
I was too terrified to move

I'd always had a fear
of being buried alive

I would dream of bells ringing
in misty churchyards at night
with no one to hear them

then I found I could move
only a little strangely
like action at a distance

and there was a world to move in
that somewhat resembled my own
air to breathe that almost tasted okay
and water that didn't

I could pass among the living
mostly unnoticed

I've heard a lot about the dead

not knowing they're dead
but from where I stand
it's the living who don't know
they're alive

from street to wind

1
I found a street
and walked along it

there were people doing
the things people do
when they're not doing
anything else

there was a dog, minding its own business
and a cat, keeping watch on the sky
and a tree with a sleeping bird

there was nothing to suggest
that anything was any different
so I didn't ask any questions

that worked until the end of the street
then there was another one

2
when I came to sit down
there were no chairs

so I sat in the middle of the air
like a saint in a Medieval painting

contemplating the worlds that spin
on the palm of god's hand
but seeing it all
from the wrong end of creation

when I got up to walk
I decided to keep
to the pathways of the sky
the gardens of the wind
the consolations of love
and the secrecies of water

to leave it all, seed and swarm
a world all torn
and find another place
to be born

3
when I came to pray
there was nothing I could say

no words to form
between formlessness
and form

no path
that wasn't too well worn

no gestures that would stay
no match between sound and sense

I had no knees to bend
no palms to clap
into a steeple
to bring the two halves of me
together

no tongue to shape the chant
that might grow in the heart
between beats

neither flesh nor feet
nor the spaces to move
from wind to street
to find a street and walk along it

you have to be dead

you have to be dead to walk among
the homeless and the starving
over the garbage dumps
where children pick and fester
across beaches filthy with plastic
and trees that gesture to memory
from dry branches

well... you don't have to be dead
but it's easier

you fit in better
no so alone

feel right at home

blood and guts

it was a dark dark night
in a dark dark place
in the darkest of times

the vampires came out to play
blood enough to go round
moon enough to dance

where vampires dance
mirrors go still

there's nothing there but shades
it's all in our heads, they say
like a moon always full
like a song that never stops
a dawn that never comes

but while
the vampires have already
gone back to their coffins
cursing the light
we stay on to the end
still killing and spilling

more than enough blood to go round

more than enough moon

to dance

traceries

looking back I can see
traces of a life
not much more

wasps and wisps

I could've made it up
or someone else could've
made it up for me

a time before this

before I died
I loved to take my fancies
for a ride
and to join them just for fun

before I died
there were worlds a-plenty
all dressed up
with words for every one

and everyone had their say

the horizon expanded and contracted
like an eye in the sky
and laughter did open commerce
with those close and far away

while children chased clouds
where clouds did fly

every stop was a start
every door was open,
every conversation a journey

every notebook entry
a tribute to an ongoing future
and every love
was a love for all time

then I died
and with heartbeat hung suspended

fancy fades
and so do I

this is where I died

If you like I can show you
where I died, the exact spot
the moment it came upon me
what I was thinking about
where my hands were placed
and what my feet were doing

even the expected is unexpected
when it happens
right out of the blue

all too soon
the world is at your door

I don't suppose, however
that geography matters much any more
even the dead want to move
to higher ground

I don't suppose the land remembers
beyond a certain point, or has to say
he died there
he was cleaning the car

and listening to the radio
some shock jock
ranting about the evils of immigrants

or she was talking on the cellphone
when worlds collided
and everybody jumped out of their skins

this, then, is where I died
right where you are
right where I said I would be

you can watch it for yourself
in real time
when the moment comes

a comet's tale

I imagine this   continuity
but when I look there is none

the more I look the more
holes appear

the more gaps open out
between things

until there is nothing much left
but a comet's tail
and the mere memory of matter

deadland

it's no bowl of cherries
over here in deadland
where the wind blows
hot and dry
from nowhere to nowhere
and seawater inundates
coastal springs
turning everything yellow
and the reservoir fractures
into a mud cake abstract

there're a lot of restless souls here
whose feet have lost the shape
of the earth
and whose faces have lost
the mask of the sky
the fit of the air
and whose minds will never be
the same again

over here in deadland
where blue has paled out of the sky
and the sun never goes away

and characters from past lives
chatter on about how things
used to be, back in the day
when they were alive
and still had a lot of loving to do
and summer green and blossom pink
would never leave the world that way
the slow fade
the desiccation of hopes

I'm sorry you had to wake up
and find yourself in this sort of company
in this sort of place
but it happens that way
you blink and the world goes away

and you're some place else
you never intended to be

the lament of the colourless

colours got drained away
hills faded
and cities turned grey

the ocean lost its blue
the air did too
and smiles were no longer scarlet

the green and yellows
went mellow
and then browned down

the mauves and purples
fawn, sepia and beige
apricot and magenta
everything with a nuanced shadow
dimmed
and washed right out

all that was vivid
turned livid
to look ashen was all the fashion

before you could say
show me the evidence
everything bleached into
grayscale
the tones of a stony riverbed
before turning inert, like lead

on the artist's palate memories swirl
into muddiness
the paint evaporates on the brush

so here we are at the gate, at the wall
hoards of us
with our grey faces and our grey eyes
and our shadowed lives
and our wan cries
up out of our earth graves
and sky graves
and the empty graves of grief

demanding our colours back

Prometheus

I'm sorry to have to say
my mind is like a leaky boat
my feet are ablaze
my heart seems unprepared
for another day's hard labour
and I've lost my taste
for explanations offered
in soft voices

you might say I've seen better days

I don't have much to offer, I'm afraid
crows have been picking at my guts
harpies picking at my mind
while the rest of my body
keeps on saying hello to death
at the dawn of every day
always blood red

I can only dream of former glories
except there were no glories
all those stories were just made up
by unscrupulous poets

looking for someone to valourise
turning me into a figure
I could never be

they say I stole fire from the gods
to give to mankind
turning me into some kind of super hero
but that's a damned lie

mankind didn't need me
to do its dirty work

you'd been nursing that fire
in your breast
for a millennium
you mad monkeys

burning all that coal
was your own idea
not mine
but I have to carry it
for reasons that are deep and strange

those gods that men bleat about
have singled me out

I have my liver torn away each day
and the rock to which I'm bound
faces the incoming tide which is all fire and ice

with a bit of luck
I might just wriggle free
but I'm not holding my breath

I'm too busy screaming

the houses of sleep

there are eyes that have never belonged
to the sky

faces that can't be found
in trees

feet that have never touched
the earth

bodies that have never known
the love of air

spider minds with no webs

aliens with no memory
of forests

while in the house of sleep
pillows gather dust

aftermath

I roll to the edge of the bed
and look over

nothing but the abyss

the sheets are crawling off
the edge of dream

last night the talk
was all about love

the body next to me
is starting to smell

the rot sets in

after a while, tiredness creeps in
limbs get heavy
blood gets sluggish
and the mind doesn't mind

you can barely bring your eyes
up the horizon line

barely bring your heart
to the wailing wall

barely bring your mouth
to the river

the world, and all in it, slips
from your fingers

you want to say goodbye
but your words have forgotten
common courtesy

and your heart already belongs
elsewhere

memory

the children play hop-scotch
jump and turn
through chalk squares

some can do it, some can't
some don't bother

the skipping girl comes by
wrists turning in a halo of rope
scattering the picnic

in a parallel world
none of this is happening
and the dead are content
to stay that way

when thinking became truer than truth

we were warned but paid no heed
we were told but didn't listen
(we thought we knew better)
the signs came and went
but we didn't see

we lost the words because
we threw them away
and when we needed them
scratched for them
we found they had been
spirited away

and suddenly everything
was in the past tense

time and again, it was pointed out
that if we didn't take action
we would lose everything
and we walked the other way

it was just cowardice, really
no wonder we are all, now,
just ghosts
wandering about in an afterlife
barely resembling the world

all the knowledge we needed
was at our fingertips
and we turned our backs
because thinking became truer
than truth

and in this way we lost our way

back in the basement

as the party parties
the shakers shake
and the pills are popped
and the air is filled
with the smell of forests

I can't help but think
of the vampire in the basement
and what will happen
when it gets loose

a drop or two of blood
in the cocktails
the fine spray of decay
in the air

I don't know, I must have taken
the wrong coloured pill

I can already hear the moans
and the bemoans
and all that vile sighing

one more hit
and I'm out of here

money mad

1
these big-shots and fat-cats
and know-alls and richy-bitches

are just cowards
when it comes to it

when it comes
to fronting up to it
fronting up to anything

they just run away and hide
and whine
for more of your money

2
nobody asks much anymore
where the money comes from

it's just money

but it can go on buying you out
until there's nothing left of you

and empty the world
before you can count your blessings

break the back of man or woman
or child
before they have stood upright

nobody asks much anymore
where the money comes from

but it would be better if we did

3
money!
money can fly with no wings
run with no legs
get rid of ghosts
perform
all kinds of magical tricks
to outsmart the gods

It's the best we have
this side of Christmas

get your hands
on as much as you can

while you can, buddy

it's said that you can't take it with you
but I don't know about that

I've seen a lot of dead people
on the move
with something jingling in their pockets

the returned

travelers from the future return
with tales of horror, war
and mass death

they are gagged and locked up
by the gaggers and lockers
the huggers and muggers

they don't like the idea of real history
or of people coming back
from the future
seeking a better death
and telling tales of chaos to come

they don't like the idea that their children
might come back to haunt them
as the hollow-eyed dead
so they do an angry stamping dance
and stamp on every face on which
the future is written

and frantically arm up
for horror, war, and mass death

endings

it used to be that you could steer your ship
by the whispered syllables of the stars
and weigh anchor
in the verses that lie snuggled
between peninsulas
and bays that smell of graveyards

you could find a safe place
between the lines
and the rhymes
of the road that leads over the hill
and around the coast
to the city of flowers
where the dead have made
a new life for themselves
in the provinces of plenty

that carefully stitched syntax
has come unravelled
because used-to-be arrived
reeking of nostalgia
like the yellow smell of broom
because the landscape

has abandoned poetry
for a life among the cinders
where there is no safe place
most of the feeling is done
in the past tense

and you can never trust
the endings
to deliver a true report

Also by Mike Johnson

Novels
Driftdead
Lethal Dose
Zombie in a Spacesuit
Hold My Teeth While I Teach You to Dance
Travesty
Counterpart
Stench
Dumbshow
Antibody Positive
Lear: The Shakespeare Company Plays Lear at
Babylon

Shorter Fiction
Confessions of a Cockroach/Headstone
Back in the Day: Tales of NZ's Own Paradise Island
Foreigners

Poetry
Ladder With No Rungs, Illustrated by Leila Lees
Two Lines and a Garden, Illustrated by Leila Lees
To Beatrice: Where We Crossed the Line
Vertical Harp: The Selected Poems of Li He
Treasure Hunt
Standing Wave

From a Woman in Mt Eden Prison & Drawing

Lessons

The Palanquin Ropes

Non-Fiction
Angel of Compassion

Children's Fiction
Kenni and the Roof Slide, Illustrated by Jennifer
Rackham
Taniwha. Illustrated by Jennifer Rackham

Lightning Source UK Ltd.
Milton Keynes UK
UKHW040719290422
402257UK00002B/370

9 780995 128224